HOW TO BUILD SELF-DISCIPLINE

21 Proven Techniques To Develop Successful Self-Discipline Habits, Skyrocket Your Productivity and Achieve Your Goals Faster

THOMAS SCOFIELD

TABLE OF CONTENTS

Introduction

Congratulations on purchasing *How To Build Self-Discipline: 21 Proven Techniques to Develop Successful Self-Discipline Habits, Skyrocket Your Productivity and Achieve Your Goals Faster* and thank you for doing so.

The following chapters will discuss 21 different habits that are conducive to establishing self-discipline into your daily routine. Self-Discipline is mandatory if you want to enhance any area of your life. If you want to improve your health, impress people in authority, earn more money, or learn any new skill, then you will need to master self-discipline.

Self-Discipline is the ability to control yourself in any situation. A self-disciplined person will be able to recognize their own weakness and then take the proper steps to correct them. Self-discipline will teach you how to think and act with proper discernment. Temptations, peer pressure, drowning in stress, and of course, practicing bad habits, can all lead to making decisions that will only cause more stress and temptations to cement into your life, and thus, lock you in a vicious circle that can feel like a prison. There is a key to free yourself from this prison of bad habits though, and that key has been in your hands all along. When you transform into a self-disciplined person, you will obtain mastery of the self. When that is accomplished, you will see that there is no longer anything holding you back from achieving all that you desire.

There are plenty of books on this subject on the market, so thanks again for choosing this one! Every effort was made to ensure it is full of as much useful information as possible. Please enjoy!

Chapter 1:
Scheduling for Discipline

Self-discipline is one of the greatest virtues that a person can aim to obtain. There simply is not a single aspect of life where having self-discipline will not be beneficial. Self-discipline is the main ingredient to achieve success and fulfillment. Without self-discipline, you will always be at the whims and mercy of other people who do have self-discipline. It has often been said that the world is not fair. Whether that is true or not is irrelevant. If the world is not fair, then it is up to you to turn the tables in your own favor. If the world is fair, then it is also up to you to remain balanced and productive even when the odds start stacking against you.

During the worst of times, you will need self-discipline to remain on your path instead of getting thrown off it. During the best of times, you will still need self-discipline to remain centered and not become too presumptuous. If you lack discipline then you may give up on whatever you are trying to accomplish too early, or your ego may grow too big and trick you into falling into a bad habit. Practicing self-discipline gives you the power to keep going even when you are about to give up, as well as stop yourself before making too big of a mistake. It not only helps you to reach a higher platitude of success and fulfillment, but it also stops bad judgment from manifesting as a bigger problem down the road.

The first pillar of self-discipline involves scheduling. In many ways, keeping a well-outlined schedule is the cornerstone of becoming, or remaining a disciplined person. There are many reasons why this is true. Having your activities set to the rhythm of a clock will help to establish good habits. At the end of the day, establishing and upholding good habits is what discipline truly aims to do. Your habits probably already, even if you don't realize it, are set to a schedule.

Habits are dictated by the human subconscious. The subconscious is in control of everything that you don't have to think about. This pertains to your bodily functions, the workings of your organs, the words you speak that you didn't mean to say, and everything else that you do which you are not in conscious control of. If you are reading these words right now, then that is the self-conscious part of your mind operating. When you do something else that you did not consciously select to do (smoking a cigarette, grabbing a snack when you are not hungry, speaking in haste, etc.) then that is the sub-conscious part of your mind operating. There will not be much more psychology covered going forward in the rest of this book, as I am well aware that the majority of people want to get straight to the advice, tips, and strategies, but let it be understood that what self-discipline aims to do is retrain your brain and replace unproductive habits with efficient and productive ones. Once these productive tips and strategies have fully entered into your subconscious, then they will become habits, and you won't have to *try* to do them anymore. They will just happen automatically. That is the power of the human mind.

Keeping a solid schedule is the most efficient way of forcing good habits into your subconscious. This may sound ironic, but keeping a solid schedule is the first habit you will have to establish to cultivate self-discipline, and it is also the last. The reason I say that is because what this book aims to do is; *help you to create a solid schedule of good habits*. Just having a schedule is not enough to become a disciplined human being. If you have a schedule of bad habits, then nothing will change. Yet, if you can create a schedule of good habits, then soon enough you won't even recognize the type of person you are anymore. The old you, unproductive and wasting time, will have transformed into a brand new person who is capable of making their wildest dreams come true.

According to current scientific data, it takes the average person about 90 days to replace an old habit with a new one. That is the challenge that is presented to you here. For the next 90 days, you are to create a schedule that focuses on practicing good habits. That is why scheduling is the first item that needs to be covered as well as the last. First, you are to write down a schedule for yourself. Second, you will start practicing the habits mentioned in this book. Then, lastly, you will aim to uphold your schedule while slowly adding more good habits into it. Do this for 90 days, and then take a look at your life. I am sure that you will see a more productive person in the mirror.

Everyone's life is different. There is no way I can know what your current routine is. That is one of the reasons why there is not much advice given in this chapter for how to arrange your schedule. Figuring out what type of schedule works for you, is up to you.

Before writing down your schedule and sticking to it, read through the rest of this book. Read about the other 20 habits, and then slowly arrange the schedule of your day around them. Scheduling, the cornerstone of self-discipline, is the first thing you have to understand before initiating the process of transformation. But, it is also the last thing you have to work on. You have to know what good habits to include in your schedule before you can begin practicing them.

Now that we have covered the concept of Scheduling, you may move on to the other 20 tips. Just remember though that after you have gone through those 20 tips, you must integrate them into this first tip of scheduling and stick to the schedule for at least 90 days to see a positive change. You can do it. I know you can because, when someone is disciplined, they can accomplish anything.

Chapter 2:
Diet

Normally, most books of this type would tell you what to eat and what not to eat. Of course, eating the right types of food is extremely important to living a healthy lifestyle. However, when speaking about cultivating self-discipline, something that often gets overlooked is the timeframes that people eat. As you go about arranging your schedule of self-discipline, knowing when you are allowed to eat, and when not, is just as important as selecting the right food. These are the two aspects of dieting that must be combined together for the diet to be successful. One is selecting the proper food, and the other is selecting the proper timeframes.

The common formula for obtaining a well-balanced diet is eating three meals a day: breakfast, lunch, and dinner. Yet, so many people do not stick to this basic formula. A major area where many people make an undisciplined error is eating too late at night or eating too much. This is understandable, and no one should feel guilty for doing so. After a long day at work, most people want to relax when they get home (which they should). One of the quickest ways to induce a sense of relaxation is to sit down with a big plate of dinner and take out your stress on the food. I am sorry to tell you, but if you want to become more disciplined then this is one of the first habits you will have to replace.

When writing your schedule make sure to allow proper timeframes for eating. No meal (aside from the occasional celebration) should ever take a half-hour to eat. Generally speaking, eating a meal should never take longer than 15 minutes, not incorporating prep time to make the meal. Set aside time for all three meals (breakfast, lunch, dinner) but do not go over the allotted time limit you have given yourself.

When you first start doing this, your stomach will rebel against you. It may whine and cry, demanding that you fill it up with more food, but do not listen to it. Only eat as much as you need to feel satisfied, and only do so for 15 minutes. Don't under eat, don't overeat, just slightly fill your belly and then move on to the next part of your schedule. If you have a habit of eating late night snacks then you will have to abolish that before doing anything else. Remember that the craving to gorge on a late night snack is a subconscious habit, and your old habits will fight you with tooth and nail while you are trying to change them. Denying cravings is an exercise in willpower. To cultivate willpower is the same as cultivating self-discipline.

To reiterate and keep it simple, only eat three times a day. Spend no more than 15 minutes per meal. Do not eat anything all day besides those 3 meals. Try to avoid extra snacks. After doing this for a few weeks (sticking to a schedule), your metabolism will readjust, and the former cravings will begin to subside.

Some people may have trouble beginning this process. Just remember that if you can make this one little change of only eating at set times, and eating set amounts, then you will begin to replace the old habit with a new and healthier one.

Something that you can do to help get you started is to replace your old snacking sessions by drinking a fluid of some sort instead. Water or any beverage with electrolytes will not entirely replace the sensation of gorging on snacks, but it will help to replicate the bad habit that your mind is already accustomed to performing. This is one of the great secrets to eradicating old habits. You still do something that mimics the physical activity you are trying to rid yourself of (in this case putting sustenance inside your stomach) but you replace the old action with a new one. The old action is eating a snack too late at night, and the new action that we are replacing it with is drinking a fluid instead. Do this at any other time of the day when you feel a craving for food coming on outside of your scheduled eating times. Besides water or electrolytes, you may also want to try drinking tea, a juice, or any other healthy beverage instead.

As for what types of food to eat, it is best to not eat carbs after lunchtime and avoid caffeine after 5 pm. Try to balance out your meals with equal amounts of fish, poultry, vegetables, meats, fruits, and nuts. Remember to keep the portions within something that you can eat with 15 minutes and try to balance out the 5 basic food groups. Also, place a highlighter over the word *fish*. It has been proven that eating at least two servings of fish a week helps to bring clarity to the mind and having a clear mind will help you to remain on the path of discipline instead of falling off it. For those out there that are worried that they can't accomplish this concept of eating by a set schedule, don't worry. You are allowed to cheat a little bit, at first, but more on that will be covered later. For now, just write down the times that you plan to eat in your schedule, and when you feel a craving coming on, drink a fluid instead.

Chapter 3:

Exercise

Let it be said right here that if you can simply stick to a proper schedule of eating and exercise, for 90 days, then you will see changes in your life. Your entire world won't change, but you will have gained the discipline to begin the process of creating the world and lifestyle that you want.

The benefits of exercising have been extolled so much that they need not be repeated in vast depth here, but a word should still be said about how great a practice exercising can be. Although it may sound counterintuitive, getting a hearty amount of exercise will help to fight off food cravings. This is because that when a body is exercised, its inner resources can regulate themselves easier. A body that sticks to a scheduled workout routine (and eating routine) will have a better idea of when it needs to save or expend energy.

Getting regular exercise will also help to regulate sleep. When energy, food intake, and sleep are all running under a routine, uniform, consistent system, the body will no longer become confused as to when it should digest, rest, use energy, and save energy. Getting into a habit of exercise alone will serve to make great strides for becoming more disciplined.

Different sorts of exercise work for different people. If you have never begun a regimen of exercise before then you may want to begin by just taking short walks every day. If you do it every day then eventually you will be able to walk further and longer than you previously could before. For those out there that feel they need something more strenuous than just walking, there are many options available. Running, or any other sort of cardio workout can do wonders to transform the body and mind. Practicing yoga, Tai Chi, or some other slow-moving form of body control won't just help to ease you into a pattern of exercise but will also help to teach your mind to become disciplined as well.

Another option available, for those that want to have a little fun while they work out, is dancing. Check around your local area to see if there are any dance classes available and sign up for one if you haven't yet.

If you want to push it even further, instead of enlisting in a yoga, Tai Chi, or dancing class, look into a martial art school. Honestly, if you join a martial arts school and stick with it then you may not even need to add anything else into your routine to become more disciplined. Martial arts are known for teaching how to fight, but that is not the true goal of any martial art. The true goal of martial arts is to teach self-discipline. There is not a single lesson taught in a martial arts school that is not secretly teaching the mind to cultivate more discipline. If you did enlist in a martial arts school, you would be gaining not just the benefits of exercise but also all the mental training techniques that help to keep you on the disciplined path.

Although the previous passage promotes martial arts, whatever type of exercise you decide to add to your life is up to you. Look into the different options and try to feel out which one you think you could see yourself doing 90 days or even a full year from now. The important thing is not exactly what type of exercise you start practicing, but that you stick with it. Write in time frames of when to exercise into your schedule. Also, keep in mind that you don't need to exercise every single day. Aim to exercise for at least four days a week, and if you think you can do more then go ahead and write more exercise time into your schedule.

One last word on exercising, and why enlisting in a class of some sort can help. Many people who just started exercising will quickly hit a wall where they don't want to continue doing it. When this happens, exercise anyway. It is that simple. Prove to your mind that you are going to do what you claim. If you enlist in a class and spend money on the exercise program, whatever it may be, then you will be more likely to begin and complete your workout even when you don't feel like it. For those very blue days where you really don't feel like exercising, lower the amount of exercise you do, but still do it. It may not be optimal, but the point is that you keep doing it for 90 days until it becomes a habit.

Chapter 4:
Sleep

Sleep should not be random. Having a set sleeping schedule is just as important as incorporating an exercise routine and eating right. In our current hectic world, many people will sacrifice sleep for something else, recreational or otherwise. This is a habit that needs to be stopped as quickly as possible. Every person should be getting 6-8 hours of sleep every night. When people do not have a solid sleeping schedule they often become lethargic and are quicker to suffer a bout of irritation. When these vices begin to take hold of an individual, they can start to underperform in several other areas of their lives. On the other hand, when someone gets a proper amount of rest, they can tackle whatever is on their schedule with gusto and determination.

Everyone knows that sleep is required to restore energy to the body. Even so, many people ignore this fact and pretend that they can get along just fine with only minimal sleep. This can be a difficult habit to alter as it has a lot to do with someone's circadian clock. A circadian clock is an inner timepiece that all living creatures have hardwired into them from birth. When someone falls into a pattern of sleeping very late at night or oversleeping in the morning, they won't be able to change this habit until they re-adjust their circadian clock. There are several tricks to making this shift a smooth transition.

Not only do you have to include sleep time into your daily schedule, but there should also be a schedule built around sleeping as a whole as well. You should have a routine that you stick to before going to bed. If you can establish a solid routine, and stick to it, then after a few weeks whenever you begin that routine your body and mind will recognize that it is time to get rest and become sleepy. As with everything else, this will not kick in right away but if you stick with it then your circadian clock will begin to reset itself. After your biological internal clock has completed this transition, sleep will naturally start to come easier.

You should begin your sleeping routine about an hour before bedtime, whatever bedtime is to you. Try to start this routine at the same exact time every night without exception. To start the process, engage in an activity that is relaxing and simple – something where you don't need to focus too much on the task at hand. Watching television, taking a bath, listening to light music or a podcast, mediating, are only a few different options available.

Most likely you already have some sort of pre-established sleep routine. Try to alter a few things about it, but also use some of what you already do to your advantage. Brushing your teeth and washing your face at the end of the day can easily be added into your sleep routine. If you already like to read in bed, then continue doing so but make sure to time your reading. Whatever it is that you enjoy doing before going to bed, make sure that you don't do it for too long. Stick to your schedule.

Sleeping aids are not recommended for resetting your circadian clock. Sleeping aids can make the person taking them dependent on the drugs, and when they are removed, the person will soon discover that they can't get to sleep without them. When this happens people will often have an even harder time sleeping afterward. Try to replace the habit of using a sleeping aid with something more natural like burning a lavender incense or drinking some decaffeinated tea before going to bed. If you exercise regularly and don't eat before bedtime, then your body should naturally fall into a state of sleep easier anyway.

Set a routine schedule 1 hour before going to bed, and even if you want to stay up and play, go to bed anyway. By doing this you won't only be resetting your circadian clock and practicing self-discipline, but you will give yourself more time to complete all the things on your schedule the following day.

Chapter 5:
Organizing

At this point, you can begin to write your schedule. Setting aside 6-8 hours for sleep, deciding when you will exercise (and what type of exercise), and eating only during certain timeframes is more than enough to get you started on the road to mastering self-discipline. Trying to change too much of your life all at once may lead to negative results. To become disciplined and stick to your schedule, it is recommended to only replace a few habits at a time. As you try to become a more disciplined person, your old habits (your old self) will do everything it can to keep things the way they are. Change can be very scary, and you have to realize that your subconscious does not know why you are trying to make these changes. To mitigate this subconscious fear, don't try to take on more than you can handle at once.

Waking up and going to sleep at the same set times on a daily basis is what the entirety of the rest of your schedule will depend upon. Eating only at certain times will not just help you to maintain your sleeping schedule, but also assist in being able to plan out the other positive habits that you intend on adding to your daily schedule. Getting regular exercise will help to teach your body when to store and expend energy, as well as even out the rest of your overall health. When combining these three principles into one schedule, you will be practicing the concept of organization.

Recall that the first pillar of self-discipline is maintaining a schedule. The second pillar is being organized. Being able to uphold your schedule will depend upon how organized your life is. If you are capable of eliminating the random, arbitrary, conditions of your life, then you will have a far easier time sticking to your schedule. These two pillars – scheduling and organizing – are absolutely necessary. Even more, they are also intertwined. One cannot be done without the help of the other.

You have to bring these two pillars together and create a solid foundation for your budding self-discipline to blossom. It is still recommended that you look through the other tips in this book, but you don't have to automatically apply all of them just yet. You should master these first concepts of eating at the right times, having a routine sleeping pattern before going to bed, and getting regular exercise before trying to add more good habits. If you can keep up these three things for 90 days straight, then they will have become habits and you will automatically start doing them without having to utilize too much effort. After you have made all of these a part of your daily life, then you can begin to start practicing the other tips.

Yet there is something else you can do to expedite this process. You don't just want your schedule to be organized, but you will also want to begin practicing the art organization in other areas of your life as well. Take a look at the things you already do on a daily basis. Try to pinpoint what is redundant or unnecessary. If possible, try to remove these from your life. Adopt a mindset of not what you want to be doing, but what you *should* be doing. Before partaking in any activity that will require a dedicated amount of time, ask yourself if there is something else you could get done that is more important or beneficial. If there is, then do that instead.

Extend this notion of practicing organization to any area of your life that you can. When at work, is everything as organized as it could be? Do you know where everything is in your home without question? Do you have all of your bills in order and know when the next set of payments is due? Do you have all of your upcoming appointments written down and have allotted proper time to execute all of them? If you do not, then placing extra time aside and going through these items is mandatory. This is a very important point. To open up more room in your schedule, you need to first whittle down on the things that are taking up your time.

Cut down on the redundancies. Remove what is not needed from your life. Minimize your distractions. Design your schedule around the idea of doing what must be done first, along with setting certain timeframes for each activity. Follow your organized schedule for 90 days straight without interruption (or at least as few interruptions as manageable). The most disciplined people on this planet all stick to an organized schedule, and they don't have time for frivolous distractions. That is one of the great truths that are hiding between the twin pillars of self-discipline. For the disciplined person, not a single second of the day is to be wasted.

After successfully integrating all the advice given thus far into your life for 90 days straight, you may begin to add the other tips in the subsequent chapters into your schedule in any order you desire. However, there is one final piece to this first arc on the road to discipline that has to be explained. The next chapter is of the utmost importance, as it is the web that will link everything already covered together.

Chapter 6:
Managing Time

On the surface, this may seem like the same thing as sticking to a schedule. There are some clear-cut differences, but the concepts are intimately connected. The schedule is your cornerstone for achieving self-mastery. Using organizational skills and removing what is unnecessary are the tools that you use to construct your schedule. Yet, without proper time management skills, you won't be able to create a realistic schedule that you can live by. The previous chapters were geared to showing you what activities to add to your schedule when first starting out. This chapter will tell you how to add these new, positive, habits successfully.

You may want to add some tools that help to make managing time easier. The most basic tool is the traditional calendar. Yet, our modern day technology offers a variety of greater options. There are several different phone apps that making logging time and sorting out your schedule a breeze. These are nothing more than digital calendars, but they come with all sorts of bells and whistles that make tracking time and remembering dates easier. Even if your schedule is not too filled up yet, you should look into adding some of these tools into your arsenal because there may be a time in the future where they will come in handy. Even if you don't wind up using them very much, the more options you have available, the more prepared you will be whenever life tosses you surprises. Trying to schedule your life in an orderly fashion can come with some pitfalls if you don't take extra care to make sure you have time for everything. The most common of these pitfalls is double-booking yourself. Pay attention to your calendar and use the modern day apps to avoid doing this. Either way, add different items into your arsenal so you can plan for the future and organize your time more efficiently.

Another area that often becomes bloated and fills up time is sifting through emails. Along with this included is scanning phone calls. As you start to become a more efficient person, the value of your time will begin to increase, and you will have to practice proper discernment to maximize what time you have to offer to others. Electronic communication has become a standard way to interact with others, but more often than not, a lot of phone calls and emails are simply not that important. Set aside some time for yourself and go through your inbox and organize it according to priority. Whatever is not important can be placed lower on your itinerary, or you can simply remove whatever topics and conversations that are no longer relevant.

Do this with your phone as well. Go through your contact list and erase all the outdated conversations. If there are any archaic contacts, old numbers that don't exist anymore, or anything of the sort, you can remove them. Make sure to go through your voicemails and erase anything that is no longer needed as well. After your phone and email are cleared you can start scanning the incoming messages before devoting too much time to them. Make sure that you read your emails in their entirety but also make sure that you don't spend too much time on conversations that don't need to be addressed right away. The reason you are taking the time to sift through your phone and emails is to open up space and prioritize whatever is most relevant to your current situation. Scan all your incoming messages and answer all of them in order according to priority. Whatever needs to be handled right away, get to it. Everything else can wait for the proper time they deserve.

When you are stuck waiting in a line at a store or sitting in an office waiting for an appointment, utilize that time. Since you aren't doing anything besides waiting anyway, why not go through all the messages that were placed lower on your list of priorities. In fact, any time you see yourself waiting for something (and you are free to use your hands) go through your phone and whittle down whatever pending conversations you haven't gotten to yet.

To the best of your ability, try to finish things as early as you can. Don't disrupt the most important aspects of your schedule, like exercise and sleep, but if there are any projects that you have to finish, it's best to get them done before the deadline is due. Handling things early is not only impressive, but it opens up more time to get to work on other things or pick up extra assignments. With that said, try to avoid being a perfectionist. If you are ever given a project to work on, it is recommended that you do the best that you can while working on it, but also know that when something is done, it's done. Being a perfectionist has both positive and negative attributes. The positive side of being a perfectionist is that whatever projects you hand in will be impressive and immaculate, but the negative aspect is that you may never finish anything at all. Don't fall into this trapping. Accept that some things will never be perfect, do the best you can, and move on to the next item that requires your attention.

Everything listed in this chapter has been mentioned to help you plan ahead for the future. That is the gift that time management can give to you. When you know where you're going and what you are going to do next, it will be far easier to remain disciplined.

Chapter 7:
Temptations

A large part of being disciplined involves denying temptations. Most temptations are rooted in subconscious habits and desires, and as such, they can be very difficult to overcome. When constructing your schedule, be mindful of trying to avoid temptations. The best way to not fall into old habits and temptations is to circumvent them entirely. To use food as an example, if someone has previously made it a habit to eat a donut every day, then they should construct their schedule around avoiding all places that sell donuts. Or, if someone is often tempted to stay up too late, they should write something that needs to be done very early into their schedule. Since temptations can be very alluring, it's best to try and avoid them all together.

If you fill up your schedule with productive and important tasks, then that will force you to offer less time to the temptations that can distract you from your goals. This is how you should treat all temptations when first beginning this process. Temptations were previously trying to distract you from doing more important things. In this case, you will be fighting fire with fire. You are going to have to distract yourself with more important things instead of being distracted by the temptations.

Later on, after you have begun to feel the empowerment associated with being disciplined, you can directly face your temptations head-on and show them that they no longer have any power over you. This can't be done too early though, or else you may make the mistake of facing your shadow before you are ready to do so. The shadow is the unconscious side of the mind that is never seen but always present. It houses the things about us that we don't recognize. It is an extremely powerful force that can't be communicated with directly. The only real way of defeating your shadow is to change who you are, consciously, and the way you do that is by changing your habits.

Consider it like this; the shadow is the unseen side of yourself that doesn't want you to change. The shadow knows that as you become more disciplined, it will have less control over you. Excuse the extremity of this metaphor but in many ways, you have to "kill" the shadow to release yourself from temptations. This is not entirely possible, as the shadow will always be a part of you, but the shadow is going to do everything it can to keep you from changing. The shadow does not want you to become more disciplined. The tools that the shadow will use to keep you exactly who you currently are will take the form of your temptations. If it helps to clarify your understanding, consider the shadow to be a form of the "devil." You must face this devil and let him know that the old you is gone now. A stronger and more disciplined person has usurped his or her essence. Once the shadow understands that the change has already happened, it will begin to back off and stop dangling the sweet aroma of temptations under your nose.

Until you are fully ready to make this all-important step, you have to first reduce your interactions with whatever tempts you. Removing yourself from temptations will give your shadow fewer weapons to fight you with, while at the same time sharpening your sword of self-discipline. While you are avoiding temptations, try to replace the time you used to dedicate to them with more productive things like exercising, meditation, learning new skills, or a hobby that you enjoy. Battling the shadow can be very intimidating, but it is also mandatory if you want to walk the path of self-discipline and mastery.

Chapter 8:
Affirmations

Reciting affirmations is an ancient psychological technique that installs subliminal messages to the human mind. In many ways, it is not too different than self-hypnotism, but not as extreme. These are done by repeating a mantra to yourself while in a relaxed and calm state. As you continue to grow into a more disciplined person, make time in your schedule to add some affirmations. They should last at a minimum of only 5 minutes but can be extended up to 10. That is one of the greatest benefits of practicing affirmations. You don't have to spend too much time on them but like everything else, if you do them on a daily basis then they will become a habit. After they become a habit, you will begin to do them automatically without even realizing it.

When beginning the practice of affirmations, make sure to keep them all brief and simple. Don't try to overcomplicate them or they won't work. When using the power of hypnotic suggestion, keep everything small and manageable. If a hypnotic suggestion is too complex, your mind will shuffle it away as excess baggage and will have missed the point of what the affirmation is trying to impress.

Below is a list of some basic affirmations that you can use to get started.

- *"I am stronger today than I was yesterday"!*
- *"My mistakes are only hinderances, not failures"!*
- *"I make correct decisions and practice proper discernment"!*
- *"I am capable of achieving all of my goals"!*

- *"I manage my time effectively"!*
- *"I complete every task that I commit to"!*
- *"Whatever I cannot finish now, I will successfully complete later"!*
- *"I am the master of myself"!*
- *"I grow into a more disciplined person every single day"!*

Before doing any of these, make sure that you are in a relaxed state of mind. Affirmations are done best with the eyes closed, or even while meditating. When practicing affirmations, you are accomplishing many different things that will help you to become more disciplined. Not only will you be installing hypnotic suggestions onto yourself, but just the act of doing them daily and not quitting will be an act of discipline all in itself.

When your practice of affirmations starts to become a normal habit, you can add an extra level of intensity to them by utilizing visualizations. It is best to visualize yourself successfully doing the things you are trying to mentally affirm. As an example, when saying the affirmation of…

"I make correct decisions and practice proper discernment"!

Visualize yourself standing before one of your current temptations. Give that temptation a visual form to represent it, and then turn away from it. Use the power of mental visualization to make a concrete image of yourself leaving the temptation behind, denying its power over you.

Another example would be when saying the affirmation of…

"I complete every task that I commit to"!

Visualize yourself crossing tasks off of a "To Do" list and writing those same tasks onto a list that has the heading of "DONE".

There are many more types of affirmations besides the examples listed above. You may also go ahead and create your own affirmations for whatever the current situations of your life are. If you are not accustomed to the practice of meditation, more on that will be covered later, but for now, just try to repeat your affirmations for several minutes. There really are no hard and fast rules to practicing affirmations, but it is usually recommended to do them after you first wake up or right before going to bed. Try to write them into your schedule wherever they fit. You can add them along to your routine before bedtime, your morning routine, or even try to do them right before exercising. Since they do not take up much time you are free to squeeze them in where you can.

Chapter 9:
Keeping Things Simple

There are certain situations where complexity will help to win the day. More often than not though, it is better to keep everything as simple and straightforward as possible. As you go about creating your schedule, make sure not to bloat it with too many things that you simply can't accomplish in one day. Your attempt to become more disciplined and create a solid, efficient, schedule may actually serve to harm you more than help if you create something that is simply unrealistic to pursue.

One of the better ways to keep your schedule simple is to make sure that you have allotted the proper amount of time for each activity. When looking to add more exercise into your schedule, most physical trainers would say that you need to exercise for 45 minutes per session to see results. Be aware that just planning out a 45-minute timetable will not be long enough though. You also have to incorporate the prep time needed before exercising, as well as log in the time it takes you to clean up afterward. Also be aware that there are many things that you don't have to do every single day. Exercising can be split into different days of the week.

There is more to this concept of keeping everything as simple as possible than just writing your schedule though. To the best of your ability, try to employ simplicity in every avenue of your life. From the routine you have in the morning all the way down to your established routine before going to bed, keep everything as simple as possible. Even more, try to keep the way you perform at work as simple and straightforward as well. Keep your interactions with others simple, avoid complex relationships – and complex people in general. As you become more disciplined you will grow into someone who is better at navigating complex and toxic circumstances. For now though, if any person or situation in your life seems to be too random or complex, gracefully remove yourself from the environment. If you already happen to work at a complex job or have to deal with complex people, you should still try to keep everything as simple as you can anyway. The rest of the world can run around like a beheaded chicken, but the disciplined person knows that there is a better and simpler way to get things done.

It has been said by many great minds that the quickest way from point A to B is by traveling in a straight line. Try to do everything you can by following a straight line instead if drifting from one thing to another. A drifter hardly ever gets anything done.

A word should be mentioned on multitasking. Although it may appear as if multitasking is a more efficient way to behave, studies have shown that it can be a detriment more than anything else. When you are doing more than one thing at a time, it is mathematically impossible to give your best effort. When your attention and energy is divided in half you are going to make a mistake, or at the very least, not hit a bullseye. Cultivating discipline leads to the growth of many different mental functions, and one of the most advantageous among these is learning how to give your full concentration to something. Concentrating on one thing at a time makes you, at least momentarily, a master of whatever you are currently working on. When you give your full attention to whatever is most prominent, you will be able to complete the task with more speed and efficiency. By doing this, you will also be minimizing the parameter of potential mistakes, and thus, not have to redo old work over again.

Keep this in mind for eating and exercise as well. It has already been mentioned that you shouldn't eat more than you need at any given time, but also be mindful to cut back on excess condiments. You only need to eat the 5 basic food groups. All sorts of extra salts, spices, ketchup, and everything else are not needed to maintain a good diet and a healthy eating schedule. For exercise, focus on specific target areas one at a time. One day you can work on a part of your arms, the next day you can focus on the lower body, and the next day you can give your full attention to a different part of your body. Slow and steady may not win the race, but simplicity and dedication do.

Chapter 10:
Incentives

I am aware that many people who have not yet begun practicing the stringent art of self-discipline may be asking themselves what the point of all this is. The point is to morph into a more efficient, productive, and successful person. However, the road to reaching that summit is filled with many potholes and challenges. If you are holding onto the belief that cultivating discipline is all work and no play, then let us banish that notion right here and now. Another one of the purposes for becoming more disciplined is to give yourself more time to play. However, it should be stated plain and directly that reaching this goal will require a great amount of effort.

In the beginning, the challenge may seem insurmountable. You may constantly feel your old temptations calling your name like a mythical siren of folklore. To be fair and honest, the average person nowadays will not be able to stave off all of their temptations at once. As was mentioned in the previous chapter, if you want to succeed then you have to keep things simple. This is going to sound counterintuitive when first read, but there is wisdom in these following words.

You may give in to some of your temptations, at first. Notice the key word is *some*. When first dieting, as an example, you can write one "cheat day" into your schedule a week where you don't have to follow the rules. Be mindful that when doing this, you will be slowing down the process of habitual change, but the reason you are allowed to give in to some of your temptations is that if you try to change too much at once, then you won't stay on this path for very long. As you become more disciplined you will be able to fight off more temptations, but only enter into the battles that you know you can win at first.

Even with that said, you are not allowed to just stop your cultivation of discipline and start playing whenever you want. The temptations that you decide to create a compromise with (before you become stronger and crush them) are to be looked at as incentives. They are earned rewards for doing a good job.

Let us return to the example of staying up too late at night while you engage in whatever form of play that you want. If you don't work during the weekends, then you may give yourself one night on the weekend to stay awake an extra hour or two (but no more) than you wrote into your schedule. This is a reward though, and only a reward. If you have accomplished everything written in your schedule the week before – or at least gave your very best effort – then you truly have earned a little more time to do whatever you want without feeling guilty. Remember though that you still have to uphold your routine before bedtime and that when the weekend is over, it is time to get back on the path to discipline.

If you deny yourself everything you once enjoyed, then you may start to suffer a bout of depression. To avoid this, slowly remove one temptation at a time. Slowly replace one bad habit with a good habit one at a time. Compromise with your shadow as you work on bettering yourself. Personal change is a slow process. It doesn't happen overnight. It takes on average at least 90 days for a temptation to completely fall away. Be aware of this. Realistic, small, changes are more powerful and long-lasting then unrealistic drastic changes that never cement into your behavioral patterns.

There is another sort of incentive to cultivating discipline. It has already been mentioned in several passages but explaining it one more time may be needed for some people. The end result of developing self-discipline will make you a more productive person holistically. When this transformation is complete, you will be reaping far more than just one or two rewards for your efforts. You will discover that there is almost nothing you can't do. Self-transformation is the hardest process a person can go through, and if they see it through to the end, whatever challenges that present themselves afterward will seem meek and paltry in comparison.

Chapter 11:
Letting Go

You will make errors. They are going to happen. Saying anything otherwise would be a lie. There will be times when you fall off the track. There will be other times where, despite your best efforts, other people or circumstances are going to distract you from completing your mission. Accept this truth. Understand that some days, or even entire weeks, will be easier than others. No one is perfect, not even the most disciplined of human beings. Grasp this concept as quickly as you can – you will commit mistakes.

Making a mistake is fine. Missing your target goal is fine. Having a bad day is perfectly normal. What is not acceptable though, is wallowing in failure. You have to let go of your errors. Do not beat yourself up because something in your schedule did not pan out the way you wanted it to. This is one of the trickier and more advanced notions of discipline. Let go of the idea that making a mistake will dictate the entire course that you have plotted. Learn to view mistakes in a different light. Mistakes give us the opportunity to show where we have made an error and offer us the opportunity to learn from them, so we can do better next time. Then, if you make a mistake again, recognize it again and continue to commit learning from the mistake. Then, if you make the same mistake again, keep committing to the idea of learning from it.

This process of letting go extends to almost every avenue of life. Let go of regret. Let go of grudges, against other people, circumstances, and yourself. Let go of failure. Learn to recognize failure as a learning tool. If you can do that – change your own personal understanding of the word "failure" – then you will be able to let go of the idea that failure is permanent. Failure is not permanent unless you select to submit to it.

Let's say that someone, for whatever reason, has completely fallen off the path of developing self-discipline. Let us assume that too many things in their external world rallied against them all at once and they just couldn't keep up with the dedicated schedule that they constructed. If this were to happen, what this person should do is, get back on the path and start over even if they have to go back to the very beginning. That may sound harsh, but we are talking about discipline here. If someone were to show this level of dedication and start the journey back from the beginning again, then just by doing that alone they are demonstrating more discipline than most people in the world have.

Letting go pertains to another area besides failure, regret, and negative concepts of similar ilk. To mention temptations again, they have to be let go of before someone can completely move on from them. People in your life that are constantly trying to drag you down need to be let go of. By saying that the intention is not to be taken as just removing yourself from these people, but to stop caring about what they think about you. This is a very important concept to grasp. Let it be understood that, at least in part, becoming disciplined is an act of selfishness. You are trying to become more disciplined to better your own life. If, after bettering yourself, you want to try and help out others then that decision is entirely up to you. Before you can help someone else though, you must first be able to help yourself.

Never, ever, allow what someone else thinks to dictate the life you want to live. Do you really think that the bodybuilder cares that some people may think him to be insane for working out so much? Do you really think that the millionaire worries what the people in lower tax brackets think of him? People who are disciplined and successful have already let go of the need to depend on another person's opinions.

Let go of everything that was holding you back before. Let go of your negative definition of failure. Let go of the need to impress people who aren't going to remain in your life for the long-term. Let go of your shadow. Let go of your past. Let go and free your hands to grab hold onto the ladder that leads to self-mastery. Let go, and by doing so, gain control.

Chapter 12:
Taking Action

There are two different types of discipline. One is passive discipline, and the other is active. Both of these have been discussed previously but they should be described individually to divulge a deeper understanding of them both.

Passive discipline is denying the habits that you are trying to change. This pertains to removing yourself from temptations, people, and circumstances. Passive discipline should be thought of as a shield. You use this shield to defend yourself from everything that is trying to distract you from achieving your goals. The affirmations mentioned earlier were another form of passive discipline. During an affirmation, you are not actively doing anything besides offering a hypnotic suggestion to yourself. Affirmations can be very powerful all on their own when done correctly, but there is something else you can add to passive discipline that will make it even more powerful. Only practicing passive discipline without taking action will only lead you so far. You won't really start seeing results until you practice both passive and active discipline.

Active discipline is your sword. Cultivating discipline and using it passively will certainly help to better your life, but you won't be able to see how powerful discipline is unless you pick up your sword and take action. Taking action requires courage, and courage is another virtue that self-discipline will bestow upon you. Courage is not the only extra virtue that you will find waiting in the wings of a person who practices active discipline though. Taking action requires something else, and that something else is called faith.

I am not talking about faith in a spiritual sense here. What is being referred to is having faith in yourself. Many people who lack self-discipline also lack self-faith, and because of this, they often let opportunities pass them by. Someone who has faith in themselves will also have the courage to step up to the plate and take a swing, even when the odds are stacked against them. Self-discipline and faith go hand in hand, and without faith, you won't have the courage to take action when an opportunity suddenly presents itself.

There are no real exercises for learning how to do this. Any time you perform a particular action aimed to induce self-discipline, like exercising when you don't feel like it, you are executing active discipline. What you can do though is measure the rate that your active discipline is increasing.

To do this, write down a list of 4 different things that you have wanted to do but have not had the courage to attempt before. These can be small and mundane things, like visiting a location that you have not been to before, or you can pick something more brazen like going skydiving. Take these 4 separate items and pick dates on your calendar 1 month ahead of the current date. For each week of the following month, jot down one of the four things that you have wanted to do but have not had the courage to yet see through. Rearrange your schedule ahead of time to incorporate these activities. When the day comes, and it is time for you to perform one of these actions, doublecheck yourself to see if you have the courage to see it through. If you do not, then you then have a choice to make. You can do the disciplined thing, and do it anyway, or you can make an excuse and jot the same thing down somewhere in the following month. Even if you keep finding a reason to not perform the activity, keep writing it down in your calendar until you finally find the courage to go and do it.

Also look for opportunities as you go about your daily routines. Although you have a schedule that you are trying to adhere to, if a blessed opportunity pops up then you don't want to let it slip on by. You are putting so much emphasis into your schedule so that you can build a solid foundation of discipline, but life will not always fit into your schedule. With courage and faith, you will learn how to say "YES" when a sudden opportunity pops up. Just remember to rearrange your schedule whenever this happens, and to prioritize every item according to its importance.

Chapter 13:
Maximizing Free Time

In the chapter about incentives, free time was explained. To avoid confusion, know that was being talked about regarding free time in that chapter was about earning more time to play instead of only working. The free time mentioned before was aimed to tell you how to add more free time to your schedule. This chapter relates to the free time that is already a part of your daily routine as it is right now.

The most disciplined of people simply don't have free time. Every single second of their lives is dedicated to some area of self-improvement, even when they are getting sleep. You do not have to go this far, as I am well aware that most people wouldn't want to live this robotically. Even so, you still have to maximize what free time you have so you garner some benefits from it.

Enjoying your hobbies and associating with friends or family is fine. In many ways that is where the true value of life comes is. Yet, disciplined people do not waste free time. They use it to their advantage. Most likely there will be several different little things that you won't be able to accomplish according to your schedule every day. When you have free time, it would be wise to catch up on whatever little things that you couldn't get done before. Free time is a great opportunity to clear out your email, phone, or just generally organize whatever may be cluttered. It is also one of the better times to plan for the upcoming days ahead or genuflect on your errors and try to see where you made mistakes (remember that mistakes are learning opportunities).

I know that many people may worry that they will never have the chance to do something besides work, organize, and plan if they become more disciplined. Like it was mentioned in the chapter about incentives, this is a fallacy. At night, before you begin your bedtime routine, you can do whatever you want. I recommend that you continue to enjoy your hobbies on a regular basis, but with one extra rule added to them. You must track the amount of time you dedicate to your hobbies. Just like everything else, your hobbies have to fall in line with your schedule. Even playtime must run under the umbrella of discipline if you want to stay on the path without hindrance.

Then there is the concept of relaxation. This is one area where you may, from time to time, be a little less disciplined. If you have met your responsibilities and don't have any projects pending, then go ahead and take a load off. If you don't make time for yourself just to be yourself, then eventually the stress will build up too much and start to tear down the tower of discipline that you have built. I won't give any advice on how to relax, as different things appeal to different people, but I will say that don't overdo it too much. Whatever it is that you do to take the edge off, practice it in moderation.

You should notice that as you become more disciplined, some of the hobbies that used to interest you will begin to lose your luster. This is a common growing pain and nothing to fret over. Be mindful that growing into a more disciplined person is a form of self-transformation. As you are transforming, you will start to see many old things in a new light.

Chapter 14:
Competition

The undisciplined person avoids and evades competition as if it were a disease. This relates back to lacking courage and faith in the self. The disciplined person welcomes competition. Competition helps us to push the envelope further. Competition forces us to think outside the box and discover new avenues of advantage. In some ways, it could even be said that learning how to compete correctly is one of the results from developing discipline.

Imagine a sport where the teams weren't giving it their all. Imagine if business weren't constantly reworking their systems and striving to outdo each other to run more productively. Imagine if every chef cooked exactly the same, imagine if every writer used the same exact tone of voice, or only wrote the same book over and over again. This would not just create a boring world, but everything would be homogenized, and no one would ever be bettering themselves. Competition is what will force you to try your absolute best. It will teach you how to dig down deep and figure out how to overcome obstacles that originally seemed impossible to surmount.

This is another piece of advice that you won't be writing in your schedule. Instead, what you should do is learn to view competition not as a problem, but as an advantage. When you compete against someone or a group, you have the opportunity to learn many things during the process. Let's say you compete, and then lose. Take the lose well, be a good sport, and learn where you went wrong so you will better know how to do better next time. On the other hand, let's say that you win the competition. You should still be a good sport, even thankful for being given the chance to compete, but the underlying principle remains the same whether you win or lose.

The victory, although something to be celebrated, is not where your focus should be after winning a competition. The focus should be on what you did correctly to lead to the victory. Winning and losing is not what really matters – what matters is what you have learned during the competition. If you lost, recognize your mistakes and make a commitment to correct them – grow from the losses. If you win the competition, then do the same exact thing. Recognize what you did correctly and make a commitment to keep your momentum going. Learn from your wins and losses. That is the secret to competing successfully. Don't be distracted by the lows of loss or the highs of victory, as both wins, and losses, are only temporal. The lessons you learn along the way, though—those are permanent. Keep this in mind at all times. Losing is a learning experience that can be used to strengthen your self-discipline.

If you have a fear of competing, then you may want to look into enlisting in a class of some sort. Martial arts can help to teach you how to learn from losing, but there are other options as well. A cooking class, dancing, or anything that you already have an interest can be a great way to begin practicing your competitive spirit. Don't go into these classes looking for enemies and picking fights. Instead, try to figure out who the best person is in the class, and then try to catch up to their level. If you can't keep up with them, that's fine. Just try to recognize where you are going wrong along the way and continue to improve the craft that you have selected. Also, take criticism in stride. If there is an opportunity to learn, take advantage of it.

Gauge the amount that you are willing to compete. Pay attention to how often you are willing to step into the ring and diligently accept a loss. If you win, don't overlook the losers and write them off. Pay attention to what they did correctly as well. There is always an opportunity to learn and grow stronger. Don't let these learning opportunities go to waste.

Chapter 15:
Admitting Weakness

Keeping in line with the thread of logic about learning from your losses and cultivating courage, you will never make a true improvement in any area if you don't learn how to recognize your weaknesses. This is another aspect of self-discipline that is very scary for many people to admit. The undisciplined person simply won't have the strength to admit that they are weak in certain areas. If this mindset doesn't change, then the undisciplined person will continue to remain weak instead of growing.

You may want to hold off on this practice until you have cultivated more courage and self-faith. This also relates to the concept of interacting and overcoming your shadow, and that is not an easy trail to walk. Ask any psychologists about "shadow-work" and they will tell you that the average person won't have what it takes to enter into the dark realm of the subconscious and learn what they need to learn. Because of this, it is best to proceed with caution when examining your own weaknesses.

You won't be writing down these exercises in your schedule either. Instead what you should do is get a pencil and piece of paper and remove all distractions for a few minutes. Turn off the phone and anything else that may avert your focus. Get into a relaxed state of mind, take your time preparing for this exercise. When you are ready, write down an old-fashioned "pro" and "cons" list. Yet, don't write the words "pro" or "cons". Instead, write down "strengths" and "weaknesses".

Write down everything about yourself that is a strength. Anything that you are good at, other people have complimented you on, or something that comes to you naturally can all go under the "strength" heading. It doesn't matter how minute or mundane your ideas seem, write them down under the "strength" heading anyway. That's the easier part of this exercise. Now, after you have finished that, we can move onto the harder part.

Write down anything you are not good at under the "weaknesses" heading. Be as honest with yourself as you can. No one else is going to see this list except you, so don't worry about embarrassment. If you have ever experienced stage fright, write it down. If you are not good at impressing the opposite sex, write that down. If you fear competition, write that down. Most likely your list of weaknesses will be longer than your list of strengths, and guess what, that is perfectly normal. Don't fall into a negative mindset as you are doing this. The point of this exercise is to show you what you need to work on.

After you have constructed the list take a long look at your strengths first. Accept that your strengths are virtues and give yourself a pat on the back. Then look over your weaknesses. Place highlights or asterisks over whichever ones make you feel the most uncomfortable. Then look over the list again and pick just one item in the weaknesses category to begin improving. Only work on one thing at a time. After you have selected a weakness to improve, write in your schedule a set time to research different ways on how to overcome the weakness.

Dedicate time to researching the weakness. After you have gained a body of knowledge about the weakness, write into your schedule set times to work on improving the weakness. Then continue to work on improving it until you have noticed a steady rate of increase. If you are having a weight and dieting problem, then you may want to start there first.

Continue to do this and cross out one weakness at a time. Every time you have overcome a weakness, transfer it over to the "strength" category. If you do this for a solid year, then the next year when you look at the list you will be amazed at how many improvements you have made. This exercise requires honesty, courage, and builds discipline.

Chapter 16:
Mentorship

Having a mentor will expedite you along the path of self-discipline. Not only will a mentor teach you more about whatever field they hold authority in, but they will also be able to speed along every exercise listed in this book. They can help you to construct a schedule that is based on priority. They can help you to recognize your weaknesses. They can help you to stay committed to the path. They can show you when you have made an error and offer expert advice on how to correct whatever has gone wrong. They will also keep you on your toes and make sure that you don't become too distracted.

The type of mentor you choose will depend on what is available in your local area, along with whatever field you are trying to learn more about. If you run into the situation where an acceptable mentor is not available, then you can look online for someone. Online mentoring has made great strides and in many ways, you can receive the same level of information and attention online that you could by meeting a teacher in person. There is still another option available to you though if getting an online mentor won't work for whatever reason.

You can instead try to find a role model. When selecting a person to model yourself after, choose wisely. Of course, you want to pick someone who has been successful in whatever avenue you are trying to master, but even more, you want to select someone who contains the virtue of being disciplined. Some people may have just gotten lucky along their rise to fame, or someone else may have done the work for them behind the scenes. Look for self-starters and people who have overcome the challenges of life. Also, try to view your role model's success holistically. If you choose an athlete to model yourself after, keep in mind that they had teammates that helped them. Also, look into their coaches and all the others behind the scenes that helped to mold the person you intend to model yourself after. If you want to model yourself after a musician, don't forget about the other members of the band, or, manager, producer, or record label. Very rarely will you find someone who has reached the pinnacle of success all on their own. Even the best in the world have had help and teachers along the way. Do not ever forget that.

If you decide to join a class of any sort, the teacher can be used as a mentor. You can also look for silent mentors in other areas of life. People you work with, friends, the physical trainer or talented chef that works at the local deli can all be minor mentors. Recognize the talents in other people and mimic their success, even if you don't intend to tell them about what you are doing.

Statistics have shown that the average person has a composite personality comprised of the 4 or 5 people that they interact with the most. Are you associating with other disciplined, successful, people? Are you looking up to people who you really aspire to emulate? If not, then it may be time to seek out a mentor and balance out your productivity. Don't worry about writing any of this in your schedule. Instead, select a craft that you want to improve upon and then seek out a mentor to help you grow. At some point, your mentor may tell you to rearrange your schedule, and if that happens, then listen to what they have to say.

Chapter 17:
Journaling

Journaling should be a part of your routine before bedtime. Writing down the events of the day will help to show you what things you have done right and what things you could have done better. If you journal before going to sleep then that will give your mind an opportunity to work out all the stress of the day and organize your thoughts while you sleep. You are also free to be brutally honest with yourself when journaling because no one is ever going to see what you have written down except yourself.

There is no correct or incorrect way to journal, as the process is personal and intimate. Yet there are some guidelines that you should try to follow when first starting out. Write down what time you woke up, all the food you have eaten during the day, and every activity that you have done. If something particularly different happened during the day, then devote extra time to describing the event. List the things that bothered you as well as the things that made you feel good. Write down every sudden thought that pops in your head. Give those sudden ideas extra examination. You are not only journaling to learn more about yourself and chronicle your history, but also to create a healthy habit of self-examination.

If you want to push this further than write about yourself in the third person as if you are describing someone else besides yourself. By doing this you will be able to get a glimpse of how the rest of the world may view your behavior and unveil a new level of understanding of what your strengths and weaknesses are. This may seem odd at first but if you keep doing it will become easier and introduce a new way to look at yourself, thus, increasing self-understanding.

The habit of journaling can instill many different positive traits. It can make you more introspective. It can help you to remember what your errors are, long-term, and make it easier to catch yourself before making the same mistake again. It will help to clear out the stress and confusion of the day. It can also relax both the mind and body, which in turn, when incorporated into your nightly routine, can let your body know when it is time to get ready for sleep.

Many of the most successful people in the world journal and reflect upon their choices every night. In many military units (who are the most disciplined people in the world), it is a mandatory exercise to journal every night. Journaling has been proven to improve mental discipline. If it was not, then the military would never waste time on such an exercise.

Before closing your journal for the evening, write down 2 or 3 good things you did throughout the day. End every entry on a high note. The last thing you should be writing in your journal before going to sleep should be something positive about yourself. Even if it is something as normal as noting that the weather was nice. Celebrate even the smallest victories, no matter how little they seem.

Chapter 18:
Dedication

Dedication is what discipline is really all about. To become more disciplined is to become more dedicated. Without dedication, you will never be able to do anything that you can't already achieve. Since discipline and dedication walk together hand in hand, some may wonder why an entire chapter would be given to dedication. The reason for this is because dedication is of the utmost importance, and unless you have a mentor, it is entirely up to you to remain dedicated at all times.

The entire system of practicing good habits will depend on dedication. You must continue to practice good habits and slowly remove the bad ones, even when your old self is doing everything it can to prevent you from changing. Dedication is what will help you go to the gym when you really don't feel like it. Dedication is what will help you listen to the advice that is given even when your ego is trying to distract you. Dedication is what will give you the reason to rise out of bed and remain true to your morning routine. Dedication is what will help you stay committed to your nightly routine even when you want to play instead of continuing working. Dedication is what you will need to discover, within yourself, if you want to reach the end of the path of self-discipline.

There is not much advice to give here for remaining dedicated. It is up to you, and no one else, to see this path through to its completion. If you stick to your schedule then you will be practicing dedication anyway, so you don't have to worry too much about adding anything else too specific. What you can do though, is add a suggestion of remaining dedicated to your daily affirmations.

"I am always dedicated, right now, and forever"!

Repeat this to yourself every morning for 3-5 minutes while performing your daily affirmations. When journaling, list any areas where you proved that you have dedication, but also write down the areas where your dedication wavered (if any) and then make a commitment to improving upon where you made an error. Ask your mentor about dedication or do research and see what your role model may have to say on the topic.

Keep going. Don't lose heart and be overtaken by lethargy. The road to self-improvement never really ends. There will be breaks and celebrations, but the dedicated person is the disciplined person. Remaining dedicated will help to boost your confidence and prove to both halves of your mind that you really are going to do the things you say.

It is up to you to complete this process. There is no else to blame. There is no hero who will do this work for you. To stay on the path of self-discipline, you must remain vigilant and dedicated. It can be done. Have faith in yourself. Try your absolute best. If you are trying your absolute best, then you will see that dedication has always been a part of you. All you have to do is let that part shine.

Chapter 19:

Forgiveness

This concept is similar to letting go, but there are some key differences. The ability to forgive those who have wronged you in the past is one of the greatest benefits that can be gained from growing into a more disciplined person. Practicing forgiveness allows you to make more allies than enemies, and by doing so, will bring you more opportunities in both business and your personal life. All too often someone will fall into a habit of not being able to move on from a transgression and let an argument or grudge get in the way of making better decisions in the future. Being able to forgive is the same as being able to move on. If you can't move on from whatever has bothered you in the past, then you will always be running in circles.

The first part of forgiveness begins with self-examination. You have to understand why someone has bothered you so greatly before you can begin to forgive them. In some cases, this will be obvious, but there will be other times when you won't really understand why someone has offended you so much. Journaling can help to teach you the subtler reasons for being bothered by someone. This may be difficult, but if you can do it then you have just demonstrated both dedication and discipline.

Being able to let go and forgive someone is one of the final graces of becoming disciplined. Undisciplined people will walk through their lives without even realizing that the actions that were done against them (in some cases years ago) are dictating their actions and decisions today. A disciplined person will recognize that even though they have been wronged in the past, when they forgive someone, they have freed themselves from the pattern of letting the past decide their future. Becoming more disciplined is to take control of your future, and a part of seizing that control, ironically, is rooted in letting go of control over past grudges and arguments.

This is another exercise that involves shadow-work. As such, get ready to practice emotional and mental discipline. There is no point to writing any of this in your schedule, as practicing the art of forgiveness is an ongoing process. What you can do though is add a parable of forgiveness into your daily affirmations.

"I have forgiven all of my enemies and wrongs that have been committed against me"!

Say this every morning along with your other affirmations. Also, if you can bear to do it, then write down a list of those that you still harbor a grudge against. Think back over these moments. Imagine having one last stand against the person who has wronged you. Imagine the scene however you want, but make sure that you end it by offering forgiveness to the person.

Remember that forgiveness is a virtue. Not everyone is strong enough to do this. Those who cannot forgive are living with the vice of a past pain. To learn how to forgive is to grow into a stronger person. With all of that said, it would still be best to cut those who have wronged you out of your life. You are to forgive them, and then move onto a higher platitude. Lacking forgiveness is for the old you. The new you will not have the time to waste on such petty things.

Chapter 20:
Silence

There are two separate aspects to remaining silent that have to be explained. They are both equally as important but require two separate definitions. The first is the practice of mediation. Meditation has been proven to increase mental clarity and focus. It has also been proven to reduce stress and regulate the nervous system. Meditation is something you should add to your schedule. Set aside at least 5 minutes a day to practice it, if first starting out. When you get better at it you can add more time to the exercise as you see fit.

If you don't know how to meditate then understand that there are several different ways of doing it. The easiest method, to begin with, involves counting your breath while focusing on nothing besides your breathing. This may seem difficult at first, but if you continue to practice it, then it will eventually become a natural practice.

First turn off your phone and reduce all other distractions. Then get comfortable. Take your time getting comfortable, as being relaxed is needed to meditate properly. After you have found a comfortable position (if you are new to this then don't worry about sitting, standing, or laying down, just get comfortable) then close your eyes. Start counting slowly up to the number 5. As you are counting, take a deep breath. Try to focus on only your breathing and counting. Then count to 5 again but hold onto the deep breath that you inhaled. After you count to 5, count to 5 again. While you are counting to 5 for the third time, exhale all the air in your lungs. Then repeat this process for a total of 5 minutes. When doing this, try to calm down your mind. You will notice that there will be all sorts of different thoughts running around in your head. Ignore them at first. The point of doing this is not just to add another exercise into your schedule, but to practice silence. When your mind is silent, you will find it much easier to quiet down the voice of negativity and temptation. After you become good at meditating, you will learn to recognize which thoughts are relevant and which should be discarded. Listen to these tiny voices, as they are going to let you know what you are really doing right or wrong.

The other aspect of silence is more social than private. While interacting with other people, try to become a good listener. Most people wait to speak instead of really listening to what others are saying to them. This is not something that disciplined people do. Disciplined people know the advantage of remaining silent and really hearing what other people have to say. If you can become a good listener then you will be able to increase your overall ability to concentrate. You will get more out of every conversation and also learn how to pick up on the subtle signs of body language.

There is not enough room in this book to describe how valuable silence really is. You must silence the mind for yourself to truly understand the power of this practice. Add meditation time into your schedule as soon as you can, and really listen to what other people have to say.

Chapter 21:
The Strength to Say NO!

To remain disciplined you must deny the disadvantageous. This, of course, relates to temptations and peer pressure, but it also relates to how you manage your time overall. You are going to have to practice proper discrimination – which means practicing proper discernment – which means telling people that your time is better spent doing something else then what they want you to do.

Becoming disciplined does not mean that you are going to take on the entire world. It does not mean that you are going to sacrifice your own betterment for everyone else. Becoming disciplined is an act of cultivating faith, courage, dedication, and wisdom. The whole point of constructing a schedule and utilizing the different exercises found in this book is to organize your time according to priority. Yet, there is no point to doing any of this if you are going to stop just to appease someone else. You are going to have to learn how to say "NO" to people. This may upset some of those around you, but that is a battle scar on the road to self-discipline.

Pay close attention to other people that are always jumping through hoops for others. Most likely, these same people live their lives in a circular pattern. The same problems present themselves over and over, and the same people step in to correct these problems. Don't be like this. Say "NO" to others. Let the world, and yourself, know that your time is valuable.

Of course, you will not be saying "NO" to everyone. You will be saying "YES" when a good opportunity presents itself, but "NO" to everything else. Proper discernment is not an easy thing to discover and practice. It is not something for the undisciplined person. It is only for those who respect themselves enough to know how valuable their time really is.

Saying "NO" can also help to increase confidence and self-faith. You don't need to impress everyone that you meet. Doing so would be a waste of time. You will only get in life what you put in. Use proper discernment to figure out where to invest your time in your life correctly. Have the strength to say "NO" to everything that takes up time and energy that could be used for more productive means.

Conclusion

Thanks for making it through to the end of *How To Build Self-Discipline: 21 Proven Techniques to Develop Successful Self-Discipline Habits, Skyrocket Your Productivity and Achieve Your Goals Faster,* let's hope it was informative and able to provide you with all of the tools you need to achieve your goals whatever they may be.

The next step is to begin organizing your schedule. With an organized schedule in hand, dedication, and the other tips mentioned in this book, you will be well on your way to mastering the art of self-discipline.

Remember that it takes the average person a full 90 days to replace an old habit with a new one. The road to self-discipline is not free of challenges, but as you grow into a stronger person you will look back at this windy path and laugh at how easy it looks. It will take time to reach that point though. Do not give up! That is the most important piece of advice that can be given. The only person who can truly moderate your development is you. If you give up, then it is all over. If you don't give up, then you will eventually win, and change. It really is that simple. It may be easier said than done, but anyone can do it if they cultivate faith in themselves and do not drift away from the goal. The start may be hard, but after you turn the corner, you will understand that every other goal you attempt to achieve after will be realized much faster than it was in the past.

Finally, if you found this book useful in any way, a review on Amazon is always appreciated!

Other Books by Thomas Scofield

Discover How To Read Faster, Improve Your Memory And Learn Any Subject In A Short Period Of Time.

The pace of life is accelerating, knowledge is constantly growing and becoming more accessible. In today's society work and school are becoming more competitive, and if you want to stay ahead, you're constantly expected to know more and more and act faster and faster. Our time however, is still the same, so how can you keep up?

Accelerated Learning may be the solution for you, because it will help you acquire knowledge and new techniques at an accelerated speed, saving you time and money and giving you an edge over your competition.

In this book you'll discover how to improve your reading speed, develop your memory, acquire new skills faster and quickly learn any subject following the Accelerated Learning strategies. Whether you're a student looking to make the most of your time, career professional looking to acquire new skills to land your dream job, teacher or employer wanting to provide job training, this book will help you develop your learning ability and reach your goals faster.

In this book you'll discover:

- How To Learn Any Subject Faster Following The 5 Phases Of Accelerated Learning
- The Benefits And Outcomes Of Accelerated Learning
- The Theory Of Learning And How It Affects Your Performances
- How To Improve Your Memory Through Repetition, Organization And Elaboration
- A 3-Step Process To Quickly Understand Any Text
- 4 Simple Techniques To Improve Your Reading Speed
- How To Deeply Understand A Text Following The Socratic Method
- 6 Powerful Tools To Accelerate Your Learning Process
- How Organizing Your Space And Time Can Improve Your Memory And Help You Learn Faster
- Complete Lists Of Additional Books And Resources On Accelerated Learning
- And Much, Much More

Discover the secrets to learn any subject faster and achieve your goals!

"Accelerated Learning" by Thomas Scofield is available at Amazon.